Getting You Re-Positioned for Success

49 Tips for moving forward after an unplanned job change

Evelyn Kaufman

ISBN: 061570896x
ISBN-13: 978-0615708966

Contents

Acknowledgments

To my Lord and Savior Jesus Christ! There is none like you!

To Grace Dyson. Fellow Coach, Friend and Sister-in-Christ. You have been a wonderful source of encouragement and support. Thanks for keeping this project in front of me. Thanks for your insight and editing help. I praise God for you!

To Patty Benton and Erin Alli. Who could ask for better Virtual Assistants (VA's)! You have been a blessing.

To Jerome Benton. Webmaster and computer guru. I praise God for you.

To Chris McCluskey. You have been a tremendous source of encouragement and support throughout my coaching career. Many thanks! God Bless you!

To my readers:

I can't count the number of people I've encountered over the months who feel like the rug has been pulled from under their feet. They were trucking along in their career only to find out that the company was downsizing, merging or closing operations.

I've designed this book with you in mind. Enclosed in this book are 49 tips to help you before you go and/or after you've gone. They fit into 3 areas:

Personal & Emotional Tips
Tips to help you deal with the personal and emotional feelings that we encounter with a job change starting on p. 5.

Financial Tips
Tips to help you ask the right questions and make wise decisions for financial matters as they apply to your layoff starting on p. 15.

Professional Tips
Tips to help you review, reflect and revise your career brand and your professional life starting on p. 33.

Start with the tips that speak to where you are at the moment. Each tip includes motivational quotes and assignments from me – The GPS Coach™!

I hope this helps you re-position yourself for a successful new season! Feel free to email or call me with updates and insights!!! I'd love to hear from you.

To your success!

Evelyn Windley Kaufman

The GPS Coach™

<u>**G**</u>etting You Re-<u>**P**</u>ositioned for <u>**S**</u>uccess!

P.S. I've included a special bonus tip #50 just for you!!!

Getting Started With This Book

This book can be overwhelming. Allow me to suggest a few ways to approach the tips listed:

Option 1:
If you are still with your company and downsizing rumblings have occurred:

Begin with Tips 1-6. These are areas you want to work on BEFORE you leave the company.

Tips 7-18 are areas you want to work on in the first 15 days.

The remaining tips are things to work on in days 16+.

Option 2:
For others, you can approach it by the categories. If Personal/Emotional is where you are struggling, tackle those tips first. Or, if financial is where you are struggling, begin there.

Option 3:
For some of you, you may scan through the document and start with those that need the most attention in your life. Start with any tip in any order.

Notes to Self
Throughout the book, you will find a space to make Notes to Self. As you are reading through the tips jot down any of your thoughts, ideas or action items.

Personal & Emotional Tips

"If I can't make it through one door, I'll go through another door – or I'll make a door. Something terrific will come no matter how dark the present."

~Rabindranath Tagore

Tip #1: Know What You're Signing For Your Severance Package

One of my "spot coaching" clients had just found out her position was being eliminated. She was at a senior leadership position and had just left a meeting about her transition out of the company. During that meeting, they handed her a document for her signature. Those she was meeting with assured her that it was just a general document that covered the terms and conditions of her departure: "Nothing major. Trust us and sign."

Know that you can ask for time to review any document you are asked to sign and if you have serious concerns, run it by an attorney. That's what my client did, and boy is she glad she did. There were plenty of things in the document to protect the company, but few to protect her.

If you are offered a severance package, be sure to clarify:

- Are the payments offered a one-time lump sum or salary continuation payments?
- Does this disqualify you for unemployment in your state?
- Other than salary, what other benefits are continued under the agreement?

From Coach Evelyn

Don't sign out of fear and intimidation. You may regret it later. Take the time to read through any document carefully and ask for more time to review it if needed.

Tip #2: Negotiate your outplacement benefits

What are outplacement benefits? These are services that companies offer their newly displaced employees. These can include career or executive coaching, education, search firm fees, and more.

When negotiating outplacement benefits, be sure to stress the benefits from the company's perspective:

- Outplacement benefits provides a positive PR opportunity for the company as well-planned outplacement packages:
    - Help employees deal with lay-offs
    - Bring employees' careers back on track (whether that track is a new position with another company, starting their own company or exploring a lifestyle/career change)
    - Help maintain the quality of life for employees and their families

From Coach Evelyn

Draft a proposal to your boss (no longer than one page) about why outplacement benefits are appropriate as part of your severance package. Be sure to place yourself in the organization's "shoes" to note their benefits (not just yours).

Tip #3: Review All Of Your Insurance

Often, we are so upset and unnerved by the change that we forget many things. This is one. And it's a big one!

The company will probably share what happens with health insurance but make sure you also ask about life or disability that may have been provided. Among other things, make sure you find out how many days are remaining before your policies terminate.

From Coach Evelyn

Review all of your insurance policies provided by your employer so you know what ends and when (and if there are any continuation options, such as COBRA for health insurance). Also ask about life or disability, if applicable.

Tip #4: Talk to your tax person

Set up a meeting with the person that does your taxes.

Go over anything about the job change that may affect your annual taxes:

- Are you receiving any lump sum severance payments?
- Are you receiving any salary continuation payments as part of your severance package?
- Are you taking your 401K package with you?
- Are you entitled to any bonuses that you will still collect on after termination?

> From Coach Evelyn
>
> Call your tax person!

Tip #5: Know Where Your Money Is

Tips for examining your finances:

- Know what your severance package entitles you to
- Review your investments
- Review your bank accounts – are there any that could/should be consolidated?
- Review all credit accounts – can any be consolidated down for easier payments?
- Put all major purchases on hold until you can easily afford them again

From Coach Evelyn

Gather all of your statements together and take a good, hard look at your finances. Do you have a realistic picture of where you are financially?

Tip #6: Take A Time-Out For An Emotional Check-Up

We're all at risk for hits to our emotional well-being every day with stress over bills, anxiety over our families, or one of the other million things bombarding us. Where are you at emotionally? Are you in touch with your feelings?

As with any major change in life, there are normal feelings to be dealt with:

- Embarrassment
- Anger
- Loss/grief
- Depression
- Stress
- Relief
- Alternating between more than one or all of the above?

As you conduct your emotional check-up, reflect on your current feelings about where you are. **Be honest.**

From Coach Evelyn

Journal about the feelings surrounding your job loss.

Notes to Self

Financial Tips

"You cannot escape the responsibility of tomorrow by ending it today."

~Abraham Lincoln

Tip #7: Develop A Budget To Manage Your Money

One of the worst things that can happen after a lay-off is trying to keep up with your current standard-of-living and realizing that you can't once you're in too deep. Before that happens, take a few hours to go through what your family actually spends on living expenses, fixed expenses and those little extras. Where can you make cuts now in order to not have as much "hurt" down the road? Some tips from frugal budgeters:

- Cut out those "extra little stops" during your day – coffee breaks, picking up the newspaper/magazine from a newsstand, etc. Many times, by planning ahead and preparing that cup of coffee at home and taking it in a travel mug or subscribing to your local newspaper or favorite magazine, you can save a lot from "stopping on the way" to pick it up.

More budgeting tips on p. 18

"If we command our wealth, we shall be rich and free. If our wealth commands us, we are poor indeed."
~ Edmund Burke

Tip #7: Develop A Budget To Manage Your Money *(Continued)*

- Remember to include emergency and long-term savings/expenses into your budget. Even if your budget is tight, putting an extra $25 (or whatever you can afford) each week into an "emergency fund" will help relieve the pressure when the water heater busts or you have a flat-tire that needs to be replaced. Savings accounts grow over time, too, and can help with those emergencies or the down-the-road major expenses (like college tuition for the kids).
- Keep track of your expenditures for a month so you can easily track where your money is going and, more importantly, where you're overspending!

From Coach Evelyn

Prepare your budget for the next six months to a year. Are you comfortable with the amounts and the cuts you need to make in order for it to work?

Tip #8: Develop An Action Plan For The First 30 Days

Losing a job can be devastating. We hurt. We feel embarrassed. We grieve. Don't let it hold you hostage. Don't crawl into your bed and try to make the world disappear. Make an action plan!

Steps for creating a personal action plan:

1. Determine your overall goal(s) for the next 30 days. Whether you have one major goal or three, you need to know what it is. Write it (them) down and keep this paper in front of you as you work on your action plan.
2. What do you need to do/achieve in order to meet this (these) goal(s)? Think of this step as the "major steps" to your major goal(s).
3. Break your plan down into digestible smaller steps / daily tasks.
4. Be sure to include deadlines for your tasks list.
5. Build in some sort of accountability for yourself – who will you tell once you've achieved one of your major steps from #2 above?

From Coach Evelyn

What are the top 10 items on your list that you need to complete in the next 30 days (prioritize these)? What are the next ten? And the next? Re-examine and re-prioritize every time you get through your list of ten.

Tip #9: Create A Daily Routine – Get Up And Dressed Each Day

One of the best pieces of advice I received when I left corporate America and starting working for myself was to treat working at home like working for a company. My friend said she would get up, get dressed and be in her home office by 8:30. She set office hours – 8:30-4:00. She took lunch every day at noon.

Your job right now is looking for a job. Approach it the same way. That's my advice to you.

Get up.

Get dressed.

And, get to work.

From Coach Evelyn

In your planner or online calendar create a daily schedule – block out time for job search, company research, networking, phone calls, etc.

Tip #10: Plan A "State Of The Union" Meeting For Your Household

While it may feel like this lay-off happened to you and you alone, every major change to one member of the family affects the family as a whole. Gather your household together to let them know what's going on. This is generally best done after you've had a short time to digest the news yourself and you have information to share.

Be prepared to share the following with your loved ones:

- ✓ Why the lay-off occurred
- ✓ What you have been given as severance (number amounts don't always need to be shared, but a general financial outlook can help alleviate some of the worry)
- ✓ Any changes to the family's lifestyle that may be happening
- ✓ Any feelings you have about the lay-off

From Coach Evelyn

What information do you need to communicate to your family? Are there any short-term/long-term changes that need to be made in family operations?

Tip #11: Mourn

Now that you know where you are emotionally, let yourself mourn. Are you familiar with the stages of grief?

There's grief around the loss of a job. And, you may experience the stages of grief. Give yourself permission to do so. Then, pick yourself up, dust yourself off and start all over again.

Stages of grief:

1. Denial – "This can't be happening to me."
2. Anger – "Why me?"
3. Bargaining – "I would do anything to get my job back."
4. Depression – "What's the point?"
5. Acceptance – "I'm okay with this life change."

From Coach Evelyn

Ask yourself: "Which stage of grief am I experiencing right now?"

Are you aware of where you are in the process?

Tip #12: Take The Chip Off Your Shoulder

Are you feeling anger over the loss of your job? Anger at your boss or the HR person who broke the news to you? Anger about how the news was broken? Anger that this has happened to you when someone else deserved it more?

Holding a grudge is like carrying a piece of luggage (a.k.a. - baggage) around each and every day. The only person you're hurting is yourself.

Do you know what can happen to your body when you don't let go of grudges?

- Irritability
- Teeth grinding
- Gastrointestinal difficulties
- Frustration
- Stress headaches
- Neck/backaches
- ...and more!!!

From Coach Evelyn

Make a list of the grudges you're holding and work each day to actively forgive the people/ situations.

Notes to Self

Tip #13: Examine If A Vacation Is Appropriate For You At This Time

One of the best ways to help a person deal with a difficult situation is to get away. If you're in a financial position to take a vacation, or even a mini-vacation, do it!

Recharging one's battery can help with:

- Your upcoming job-hunt
- The stress of a job transition into a new position
- Your family's adjustment time to a job change
- Your stress level
- Your grief schedule
- …and more!

From Coach Evelyn

Take a good look at your finances and determine whether you have enough saved to not only afford a vacation (even a short one), but also to justify it.

Tip #14: Figure Out How And When To Tell Your Friends And Extended Family

While household members should be told immediately, extended family and friends should be told soon after. Not only will it help to have support from them, they may be able to help you find a new job or a new path.

Some tips for softening the blow:

- ✓ Tell the truth. Give as much detail as you can about the who, what, where, when and why. People tend to panic when there are unknowns in life. Think about what you think would be helpful for them to know about the situation. Draft a "speech" to reflect this.
- ✓ Change is hard on people – acknowledge that they may have feelings about this change, too. Even if it's as simple as them feeling sad for you and your household for this major change.
- ✓ Lay out your plan of action for the future.

From Coach Evelyn

Schedule a "new challenge" or "new adventure" party or dinner in order to break the news.

Tip #15: Plan Out How To Answer Questions From Those Outside Your Immediate Circle

Everyone has questions. Sometimes, they won't wait for your answers. They have an answer for you. Don't feel like you have to have an answer for every question.

And don't feel like you have to tell everyone all your business.

Figure out how to avoid the questions you don't want to answer and how you can answer those you feel comfortable answering.

From Coach Evelyn

What things should I respond to? What things are off limits? Have a "script" set up for the questions you know will come up.

Tip #16: Get Organized

Organization helps on many levels after a major life event:

- Organization can be very calming – putting chaos into order.
- Organization can help you settle on future goals and objectives for your life.
- Organization can help you get rid of the clutter in your life.

From Coach Evelyn

What organization project have you been putting off? Your home office? Your bedroom?

Get on it!

Tip #17: Identify Your Priorities

Too many times we get so busy running through life and dealing with daily crises that we forget to keep our priorities in mind. Are you in touch with what you want? Have you lost sight of what you want in the day-to-day rush of families/kids, errands and work?

While this lay-off may not feel like it, you've been given a gift. A gift to re-examine your priorities and plan accordingly.

- Maybe you have a favorite park or lake you can go to and reflect.
- One of my clients scheduled his half-day personal planning retreat at a local coffee shop.
- Another friend schedules a one day a month for planning and reflection and uses a friend's cabin

From Coach Evelyn

Schedule a retreat for yourself.

Tip #18: Review Or Create Your Personal Mission Statement

I can't think of a company that doesn't have a mission statement. Its mission statement gives them focus and direction. A sense of purpose.

Do you have a personal mission statement? If so, this is a great time to revisit it. Make a revision if needed.

If not, it's important to develop one. It will help you stay on track and help you know what to say yes to and what to say no to. According to Laurie Beth Jones, author of The Path: Creating your Mission Statement for Work and for Life, a good mission statement acts as both a harness and a sword - harnessing you to what is true about your life, and cutting away what is false.

From Coach Evelyn

I've included a worksheet to get you started on your mission statement. (Flip to the **worksheet section** in the back of this book.)

Notes to Self

Professional Tips

"Life is too short

to be little."

~Benjamin Disraeli

Tip #19: Create A New Vision Statement What Do You Want To Be, To Do, To Have?

Now that you are clear on the "what" (your mission), it's time to work on the "how" (your vision).

How will this look in your life? Your vision is a snapshot of the future with all the details and descriptors needed to bring it to life.

From Coach Evelyn

I've included a worksheet to get you started on your vision statement. (Flip to the **worksheet section** in the back of this book.)

Tip #20: Consider: Is It Time To Reinvent Yourself?

I remember when a friend of mine and I were doing a workshop. We were talking about goals and how, in order to accomplish them, there needs to be a series of steps toward it. He shared a story about how he wanted to go back to school years ago and get his masters degree in counseling. And, when he thought about it, all the reasons why he shouldn't came up. The biggest one was that the program he most wanted to participate in was in another city, 90 miles away. And, if he started in that program, this also meant that he could only take 1-2 classes at a time. That would take about 8 years, his gremlin reminded him. But, he decided to step back and ask a different question. He thought, "You know I'm going to spend the next 8 years doing something. Why not spend it doing something toward my dream?" So, he enrolled in the program and drove 90 miles once a week. That was 15 years ago. He's been in private practice ever since. He could have listened to his gremlin, not done a thing, and woke up 8 years later on the "same-old-same-old" track.

"Let our advance worrying become advance thinking and planning."
~ Winston Churchill

Tip #20: Consider: Is It Time To Reinvent Yourself? *(Continued)*

Here are some questions to get you started:

- What is it costing me by continuing on this career/life track?
- If things stay as is, what will be different in my career/life a year from now? Will I be pleased?
- What action, essential to my success, am I most afraid of tackling?
- What additional information do I need?
- What new things should I explore?
- What should I give myself permission to do today?
- Is what I am doing right now life affirming or life numbing?

From Coach Evelyn

Remember my suggestion in Tip #17?

These are great questions to process on your personal retreat or during your quiet time!

Tip #21: Adjust Your Comfort Zone

While we're on our journey, we very often get firmly entrenched in our ruts. Okay, maybe "ruts" is a little harsh, but we all hit a comfort zone that is uncomfortable to get out of once we're there.

What makes you uncomfortable?

- ✓ Volunteering at a homeless shelter?
- ✓ Talking to a stranger?
- ✓ Picking up a little something like a cup of coffee or a salad for your child's teacher?

More often than not, doing something out of our comfort zone not only opens us up to new insights and perspectives, but allows us to learn a great deal about ourselves.

From Coach Evelyn

Do at least one thing today out of your comfort zone – talk to a stranger, go out of your way to help someone you wouldn't normally. Stick your neck out!

Tip #22: Become A "Big Thinker"

Earlier in this book, I encouraged you to think up a new goal (or a few) for your action plan… As you're dreaming up new goals for yourself and your life, don't be afraid to think big – especially if you weren't happy with where your career was headed or the industry you're in.

Do you think these great events in American history could have happened without big thinkers?

- ✓ The Declaration of Independece signing in 1776
- ✓ The Constitution and Bill of Rights becoming ratified in 1789 and 1791 (respectively)
- ✓ The Wright Brothers taking their first "flight" in 1903
- ✓ The Model-T Ford becoming available in 1908
- ✓ American women winning the right to vote in 1920
- ✓ The Civil Rights Act of 1964
- ✓ Neil Armstrong walking on the moon in 1969

From Coach Evelyn

Journal about your
BIG DREAM.

No boundaries/restrictions –
what is the biggest you can be?

Tip #23: Have Faith (In God And In Yourself)

My husband Gerald often talks about staying tuned into his favorite radio station W-G-O-D. It broadcasts twenty-four hours a day, seven days a week.

Is God speaking to you during this time?

Is He trying to get your attention about something?

Tune in and see what He has to say. He will offer wisdom, guidance and direction. Through Him you will grow in confidence and strength!

> From Coach Evelyn
>
> Ask God to guide you to the scripture that you can claim during this season. Memorize it, write it on a note card for your bathroom mirror, car dash or wallet.

Tip #24: Keep At It - Persevere

This is coming about halfway through this book because lethargy usually hits after a few weeks of being at home after a lay-off. You've sent out some feelers about new jobs, you've organized and cleaned everything that needed it, you've done a lot of the items on your to-do list... What now?

Now is the time to keep plugging away – at life and at the tips in this book. Keep working on your action plan. Keep working away at finding a new job or a new life.

From Coach Evelyn

Re-examine your action plan from earlier in this book – check off what you've completed and re-prioritize your remaining "to-do" items.

Tip #25: Embrace The Stress

While stress does contribute to headaches, indigestion, relationship problems, depression and more, not all stress is bad – a lot of how it affects you is how you allow it to affect you. Embrace the stress that this new challenge in your life has created.

Good uses for stress:

- Allows drive behind your daily to-do lists and activities - Where would we be going without all of these things to do?
- Gives us a purpose for our lives – What would we do without these balls to juggle?
- Gives us something to talk about – Who doesn't complain about the people/situations causing them stress?

From Coach Evelyn

What is one way you can embrace your daily stress today?

Tip #26: Stay Focused On Your Major Goal

You have your activity plan for the next few weeks with your major goal as the "headline."

Stay focused on that goal.

Each time an additional "to-do" item pops up on your list, ask yourself if it contributes to that goal. If it doesn't, and if it doesn't really "need" to be done, scrap it.

From Coach Evelyn

Take a look at your to-do list. Remove any items that don't contribute to your major goal(s).

Tip #27: Use Your Gifts And Talents

What natural strengths and abilities do you have? Is it art, music or mathematics?

What do people often say about you? Are you the go-to person when things need to be organized? Are you the one that people run to when there is a crisis? Are you gifted at customer service?

Make a list of your God-given talents, gifts and abilities. What can you do that no one else can?

From Coach Evelyn

Think about the gifts and talents that have sparked the most feedback in your life. Did you capitalize on that during your career? If not, what needs to happen in your new career?

Tip #28: Be Optimistic

First, and most likely the most important reason to stay optimistic; no one likes to sit across their desk from a "sad sack" who came in for an interview. In order to display our best selves in these situations, it's imperative that you keep on your "best face" to land that new job!

Other reasons to stay optimistic through this transition:

- ✓ Know that this is all part of God's plan for you and your family
- ✓ People will want to be around you more if you're positive through this – which results in more life opportunities for you
- ✓ Your health will be better if you stay out of the depression hole

From Coach Evelyn

Have you slumped into a negative place? What can you do to turn this around?

Notes to Self

Tip #29: Practice Wellness

Many people polled in a survey at the end of 2005 stated that the one area of their life other than career that they struggle with is fitness and health. Chances are, if you're looking in the newspaper and online at job ads, sending out emails to your professional contacts and treating your job-hunt as your new full-time position, you've spent a lot of time sitting as you work through these steps. It's time to get off your, um, chair! Why exercise?

- ✓ Reduces risk of heart disease
- ✓ Reduces risk of high blood pressure
- ✓ Reduces risk of high cholesterol
- ✓ Reduces the risks of some types of cancers
- ✓ Reduces the risk of diabetes
- ✓ Reduces body weight
- ✓ Builds and maintains healthy muscles, bones and joints
- ✓ Reduces depression and anxiety
- ✓ Improves psychological well-being
- ✓ And... it can actually help you with your focus, creativity and performance!

More wellness tips on p. 48

"In the book of life,
the answers aren't in the back."
~ Charlie Brown

Tip #29: Practice Wellness *(Continued)*

Not only do you need exercise to be truly well, you also need to take time to renew yourself spiritually. Information from the American Academy of Family Physicians states that research shows things such as positive beliefs, comfort and strength gained from religion, meditation and prayer can contribute to healing and a sense of well being.

Improving your spiritual health may not cure an illness, but it may help you feel better, prevent some health problems and help you better cope with illness or death. Some things you can do to recharge spiritually:

- ✓ Bible study
- ✓ Prayer
- ✓ Meditating
- ✓ Singing devotional songs
- ✓ Reading inspirational books
- ✓ Taking nature walks
- ✓ Journal writing

From Coach Evelyn

Incorporate a health and wellness activity into your day. Select an item from the list above or create your own Do something to renew and recharge yourself mentally and physically.

Tip #30: Consider: Is This God's Timing For Me To Take That Career Change I Was Thinking About?

The world and the economy are both changing drastically. Is your career quickly becoming obsolete?

Consider these labor statistics that were highlighted in one of my past newsletters:

- ✓ We are moving from a **manufacturing** based economy to a **knowledge** based economy. We've seen this writing on the wall already! Because of this transition, a post secondary education is **critical**.
- ✓ The USA has 45 million jobs for which we don't have Americans with the skills to fill.
- ✓ Two-thirds of future jobs will require some post secondary education.

"Once we rid ourselves of traditional thinking we can get on with creating the future."
~ James Bertrand

Tip #30: Consider: Is This God's Timing For Me To Take That Career Change I Was Thinking About? *(Continued)*

- ✓ The numbers of men and women in the labor force will grow, but the number of women will grow at a faster rate than the number of men.
- ✓ Also, as more women enter the labor force, demand for childcare services is expected to grow.
- ✓ Goods producing industries in 1940 - 38%; in 2014 - 18%
- ✓ Service producing industries in 1940 - 62%; in 2014 - 88%
- ✓ Education and healthcare make up the fastest growing occupations between now and 2014.

From Coach Evelyn

Take the time to really step back and think if this would be a good time for a career change? Can your family handle the adjustment (financially and otherwise)? Would any additional education or training be required?

Tip #31: Complete A Skills Assessment – What Transferable Skills Do You Have?

No matter what industry you hope to get into or continue your professional development in, you've got skills from your past experiences that they can use – project management, customer service, problem solving, organizational, and the list goes on.

What are yours?

From Coach Evelyn

I've included a worksheet for you to complete in the Worksheet Section in the back of this book.

Tip #32: Get Advice From An Expert

Many people lose their jobs and have a plan in place within hours. They are focused, motivated and determined. For others, it may seem like you are taking five steps forward and three steps back. Nothing is working and no opportunities are coming your way. This may be the time to seek help. It doesn't mean anything is wrong with you. It means something's right with you! You have the wisdom and insight to seek help to accomplish your goal. Top-notch leaders do this all the time.

Some advice from career coaches:

- ✓ First and foremost, keep a positive attitude during your job-hunt.
- ✓ Be diligent when job-hunting – Have a set number of resumes that you want to send out each day. In order to customizing your "master resume" and corresponding cover letter to that position and organization, you won't be able to send out too many per day. Three to five a day is a good number to aim for when you're applying for entry to mid-level positions. Higher organizational positions may not have as many openings, but you should try for at least one a day – even if it's not in your geographical area or desired industry.

*"Be strong enough to stand alone,
smart enough to know when you need help,
and brave enough to ask for it."*
~ Author Unknown

Tip #32: Get Advice From An Expert *(Continued)*

- ✓ Prepare for interviews – You can get lists of potential interview questions in many HR books available today. Write out the questions and your answers and practice your answers out loud until they don't sound rehearsed but they do sound prepared and confident.
- ✓ Know your talents well – You should be able to list 8-10 things you do well professionally while you're job-hunting. This will be asked over and over again.
- ✓ Know yourself – You will need to be able to tell your story a few different ways in order to answer the dreaded "Tell me about yourself" question.

From Coach Evelyn

If you don't have a clue where to start or if you've been trying for months and nothing is happening, seek out advice from a career coach.

Tip #33: Update The Résumé

Get your résumé ready to go. Make sure you showcase your transferable skills. When you list the responsibilities of your past jobs make sure it showcases results and accomplishments.

Tips for a great resume:

- ✓ Be concise. No one wants to read pages and pages on you. You should be able to condense your knowledge and experience down into one page per decade of life experience.
- ✓ Be clear. Don't use jargon specific to your industry.
- ✓ Write your resume when you're in a good mood.
- ✓ Put a head shot in the upper right-hand corner to put a "face" to your experience.
- ✓ Instead of an objective section, start with a strengths section. Highlight 2-3 strengths, including quotes from past employers' reference letters, record-setting achievements, or anything else to set you apart.

"Trust in the LORD with all your heart
and lean not on your own understanding;
in all your ways acknowledge him,
and he will make your paths straight."
~Proverbs 3:5-6

Tip #33: Update The Résumé *(Continued)*

Things to leave off of your resume (actual resume blunders):

- ✓ "Accomplishments: completed 11 years of high school"
- ✓ "Graduated in the top two-thirds of my class"
- ✓ "Here are my qualifications for you to overlook"
- ✓ "I can type 25 words per minute"
- ✓ "I am seeking an entry-level position"
- ✓ "I realize that my total lack of appropriate experience may concern those considering me for employment"
- ✓ "It's best for employers that I not work with people."

From Coach Evelyn

Dust off your resume and update it with current achievements. Be sure to proofread!

Tip #34: Brush Up On Any Skills That Are Lacking

What's missing on your skills list?

It's probably just a class away. If it's computer skills, that can be tackled at a community center or community college. It may be able to be tackled by taking an online class.

Determine what you need and make plans to address it.

From Coach Evelyn

Find one class you can take that will complement your current skill set and make you more attractive professionally.

Tip #35: Develop Or Revise Your Career Brand

What distinguishes Starbucks, Target, Harley Davidson and others from their competitors? Their brand.

A brand is defined as a combination of tangible and intangible characteristics that makes it unique. A brand is a company's image – with results to match.
Your career brand should let people know who you are, why you are great and what sets you apart from the others.

From Coach Evelyn

Take time to look at your accomplishments from past jobs, education and training. Make a list of the "value" you bring to the table based on your career path so far. If you find that there's not much that sets you apart, begin to think about what skills and expertise you need to develop.

Tip #36: Brush Up On Your Interviewing Skills

With so many people looking for jobs, being a strong interviewer is a MUST. You may think you do a good job, but how can you be better? Make the time to develop strong interviewing skills.

What are some things you can do to get the best interview experience?

- ✓ Prepare ahead of time – research the company and the position.
- ✓ Role play your interview – have a friend/family member ask you common interviewing questions and plan your responses based on the organization's needs
- ✓ Practice great eye contact
- ✓ Stay positive – especially about past employers!
- ✓ Do your homework on the organization. Prepare questions about the organization – make sure they're strong questions!

From Coach Evelyn

Find an interview buddy who you can role play with for specific interviews.

Tip #37: Keep An Eye Out For Opportunities

Are you a reader? If not, become one.

Opportunities can often be found in the business section of the newspaper and business journals in your industry or field of interest.

This is where you can find out what direction companies are moving in, who is expanding or who is taking on new projects. This will give you additional ideas of places to network and conduct informational interviews.

From Coach Evelyn

Take fifteen minutes a day and read the business section of your paper or some other business news publication. Look for opportunities.

Tip #38: Develop Your Elevator Speech

I've heard people refer to elevator speeches as the "swiss army knife" of job-search tools. Why is this so important? Most of the time, you have just seconds to make an impression of yourself when you're meeting an interview or a networking contact. Not a lot of time! It's imperative that you spend those precious seconds creating a lasting impression.

What should your elevator speech be/include?

- ✓ Your elevator speech should be conversational and natural, NOT stilted, over-rehearsed or "canned."
- ✓ Your elevator speech should be memorable and full of your personality. It should never leave the other person with a "so what?" when you've finished.
- ✓ Your elevator speech should include a "hook" – something to prompt the listener to ask questions and keep the conversation going.
- ✓ Your elevator speech should not ramble – it should be concise and to the point – nor should it be sped through with no breaks for breathing.
- ✓ Your elevator speech should include EYE CONTACT and a SMILE.

"A wise man will make more opportunities than he finds."
~Francis Bacon

Tip #38: Develop Your Elevator Speech *(Continued)*

- ✓ Your elevator speech should not include jargon or other industry terms that may not interest your listener.
- ✓ Your elevator speech should include an easy "wrap-up" that you can cut to if your listener's eyes glaze over halfway through.
- ✓ Your elevator speech should include different versions for different audiences and/or situations.
- ✓ Your elevator speech can include specific stories or examples – as long as you can keep them brief and anecdotal.
- ✓ Your elevator speech should focus on how you can benefit employers and be a solution-provider for them.
- ✓ Your elevator speech should end with an action request – ask for a business card or an appointment for an interview.
- ✓ Your elevator speech should never be out-of-date – keep polishing it!

From Coach Evelyn

Develop 1-3 versions of your elevator speech for networking and job-hunting. Practice these every day until you feel comfortable with the language and changing them as needed in different situations.

Notes to Self

Tip #39: Polish Your Image

Imagine for a moment two different people going in to interview for a finance position at a bank...

One is dressed in a nice, pressed suit; has taken the time to do her hair and nails; has worked on her interviewing skills and practiced answers for common questions; and has questions prepared for her interviewer about the bank.

The second is dressed in jeans and a dirty t-shirt; her nails are cracked and chipped; her hair is messily pulled back in a ponytail; and she doesn't even bring a copy of her resume for her interviewer, much less have any questions prepared.

Now, this is a worst-case example, but you see what we're getting at here. What do you need to do to portray the right image?

From Coach Evelyn

Ask some past co-workers or professional acquaintances what they think of your professional appearance. Based on their feedback, adjust your image.

Tip #40: Identify Your "Starter Network"

We all have people in our lives who we've helped or who we know can help us with our professional goals. Do you have your list ready if/when you need it?

From Coach Evelyn

Make a list of the top 10 people you need to begin to network with.

Tip #41: Identify Networking Opportunities

ExecuNet states that building and maintaining a personal community is critical to career success. Executives agree. Eighty-five percent (85%) of successful executives agree that having a wide network of meaningful connections is mission-critical.

How do you begin? Start with business and professional peer group networks. Internally, it can range from project teams, to process improvement teams, to company service project teams. Externally, it should include professional associations ranging from accounting associations, MBA associations, young professional associations, business networking groups, chamber of commerce, rotary clubs and the like. Also consider external associations via church, community activities, and your volunteer work with non-profits. Don't forget family, friends, and even your hair dresser! They know everyone!!!

More networking tips on p. 66

*"We are what we repeatedly do.
Excellence, then, is not an act, but a habit."*
~ Aristotle

Tip #41: Identify Networking Opportunities *(Continued)*

According to Lauryn Franzoni, Vice President and Executive Editor of ExecuNet's Center for Executive Careers, people are also beginning to create personal networks via online communities with those in their same field. People tend to know people like themselves. Join a targeted community - it will increase your odds of finding relevant connections, build your reputation with that audience, and keep you well-informed of the issues, attitudes and key people.

From Coach Evelyn

Make a list of the top 10 places you can begin networking.

Tip #42: Conduct Internet Research On New Companies Or Industries

There is a wealth of information on the internet.

You can learn what companies are up to, what others think of organizations and how they rank in their industry. This can also help you learn who the leaders are.

These are the ones you may want to begin to network with or conduct an informational interview with.

From Coach Evelyn

Become your own personal R&D department. Take a few minutes each day and browse corporate websites – especially their company news/press release section.

Tip #43: Using Informational Interviews

Informational interviews are a wonderful way to network and learn more about a job or company you have an interest in. These interviews are an invaluable source of occupational information. It is a way to learn firsthand about the work involved in your area of interest by talking to people who are currently in that field.

Informational interviews are wonderful tools because…

- You get to expand your professional network with mid- or higher-level personnel.
- You gain confidence for your actual interviews.
- You get access to the most up-to-date career information – straight from the horse's (er, employer's) mouth.
- You hear about the realities of employment with that organization and the needs of that specific employer.

"I can do everything through him who gives me strength."
~Philippians 4:13

Tip #43: Using Informational Interviews *(Continued)*

- You control the interview since you're only asking for information and not a job.
- You get to explore careers and clarify your own professional goals.
- You gain an opportunity to identify your professional strengths and weaknesses.
- You can learn about "hidden opportunities" (jobs that haven't necessarily been openly advertised for that organization).

From Coach Evelyn

Make a list of the top ten people or organizations you need (or want) to conduct informational interviews with.

Email Evelyn for a free informational interview guide!

Tip #44: Consider The Possibility Of Starting A Business Or Becoming A Consultant

As a coach, I am forever in search of life-transforming questions ... questions that will wake up, shake up, and usher in answers ... answers that will help stir the mind, soul and spirit, get hold of new truths, experience new freedoms, and surprise us in achieving what we thought was not possible. In that regard, I recently spoke to a new "solo-preneur" who remarked, "If someone would have told me a year ago that I would be doing what I'm doing today, I wouldn't have believed them. This is like a dream come true."

If you've found yourself downsized or "RIF-ed" as a result of the economy, it may be just the time to dust off those dreams of running your own show. The following questions will help in that regard. What dreams do you wish would come true for your business? What do you think is not possible that you wish was possible? (Even if you're not an entrepreneur or don't have entrepreneurial aspirations, I encourage you to consider these questions, because many will be pertinent toward enjoying career success!)

From Coach Evelyn

Take some time today to think about striking out on your own. Is this good timing? Are you prepared for the entrepreneur's lifestyle?

Tip #45: Use Online Networking For Your Job-Hunt

When you are job-hunting, realize that the companies you are interviewing with are likely Googling you just like you Googled them to do research before your interview. Social networking sites like Facebook (FB) and LinkedIn (LI) come up pretty high in the results when you search for an individual. In addition to sites like FB and LI, you should look for industry-specific social networking sites to include your profile on – for example, a Virtual Assistant can place their profile on FindVirtual.com, i-Meet for event managers and InsuranceNetworking.org for the insurance industry. These are just a few examples of industry-specific sites.

More online networking tips on p. 72

From Coach Evelyn

Go through your existing social networking profiles and make sure they're all "cleaned up" and professional. If there's something on your profile that you would be ashamed to point out yourself in a job interview, remove it.

Tip #45: Use Online Networking For Your Job-Hunt *(Continued)*

What should you include for your social networking profile – and what should you leave off?

- Include any recommendations (LinkedIn has a wonderful recommendations tool where other people can write them and post them to your profile – all you have to do is request them)
- Leave off cursing, bad grammar, risqué photos and anything else that would paint you in a negative light. If you already have a profile that includes this, clean it up – chances are they will easily find anything you'd rather "hide" in a quick search on you.
- Include any travel or anything else in your images and photos that would help to highlight or showcase your interests and talents.
- Clean up your friends list. Many employers are now using social networking friends lists as the reference lists for their interviewees. They will contact the "friends" to see how well they know that person and how that person is viewed by their "friends."
- Include your past work history and your accomplishments
- Do not post anything bad about a company, an interviewer, or an interview. This will inevitably be viewed by the very person that you don't want to see it.

Tip #46: Consider A Part-Time Job

Don't be afraid to think outside of the box for this new chapter of your life!

I had a coaching client who was unable to find a full-time job in her area of expertise, but ended up with two part-time jobs. Instead of saying "No" because it was not full-time, she said yes to both. She enjoys both positions, she enjoys the variety of work, and she is meeting her financial needs.

What can part-time work do for you?

- Part-time work can help you keep your skills and mind sharpened.
- Part-time work can help you with networking contacts and to hear about other potential opportunities in the industry, or even within that same company.
- Part-time work can help to build your resume.
- Part-time work in a new industry can be a wonderful stepping stone to a new career path in a different industry.

From Coach Evelyn

Don't discount the part-time work section in your newspaper. Look to see if any professional opportunities exist in your chosen industry or in one you're interested in exploring.

Tip #47: Make A Difference

What sense does giving while you're waiting make?

Plenty.

While you are waiting for your next opportunity, volunteer.

It may only be a couple of hours each week, but it removes you from your situation for a moment. You will also learn about yourself. And, it's a good way to network. There are many volunteers who have turned into full or part-time staff. Just because they decided to give in the midst of their down time.

From Coach Evelyn

Do you have an organization in mind for volunteering? What organizations in your community are looking for help?

Tip #48: Adjust Your Thinking

Don't let your gremlin (that inner voice, critic) convince you that you have nothing to offer or are of no value to another organization. What affirmations do you need to create to alter any stinkin' thinkin'?

From Coach Evelyn

Write down 3-5 affirmations to chase away your "stinkin' thinkin'" and paste it to your mirror where you can see it every morning and every night.

Tip #49: Change Things Up

Athletes do this all the time… If the pitcher feels like the person at bat is on to them, they make an adjustment. A coach calls a time out and changes the play.

You are your own "coach" here – it's your job to be observant and do the same. Are things getting stale? Have you taken the time to really look at what you've been doing? Where can you change what you've been doing in order to yield different results?

From Coach Evelyn

Conduct a career check-up and see what needs to be tuned-up or what needs to be changed.

BONUS Tip #50

AND FINALLY... ***Get Moving! Doing "nothing" is <u>not</u> an option!***

If you are not careful, you can end up in a cycle of inactivity. You'll look up and six months will have passed and you'll still be going around in the same circles and you'll be disappointed that you haven't made any progress.

"If we wait for the moment when everything is ready, we shall never begin."

~Ivan Turgenev

From Coach Evelyn

Set goals. Each day take action toward those goals.

While you are waiting for your next opportunity, volunteer. Serve others while you wait.

Notes to Self

Worksheets

" Learn to get in touch with the silence within yourself, and know that everything in life has purpose. There are no mistakes, no coincidences, all events are blessings given to us to learn from."

~ Elisabeth Kubler-Ross

GPS Tool for Tip #18: Mission Statement Worksheet

Your mission is the "what" of your life. What you are about. It should be short, targeted, brief. I recommend the format designed by Laurie Beth Jones (The Path). key components include:

- ✓ a single sentence in length
- ✓ a core value (a word that captures the essence of who you are - i.e., truth, integrity, authenticity, wisdom, etc)
- ✓ action word(s) - verbs
- ✓ tribe (or circle of influence) -this is optional

My personal mission statement:

____

____

____

____

____

Some of my favorite mission statements:

- ➢ to restore compassion in myself and others
- ➢ to stimulate wisdom
- ➢ to communicate, motivate and promote integrity to those who cross my path
- ➢ to promote authenticity
- ➢ to demonstrate and provide excellence to business leaders

GPS Tool For Tip #19: Vision Statement Worksheet Looking Toward The Future

Your vision is a picture of your future. It's what you envision for your career. Write it with lots of descriptors and details. Write it in the present tense as if it has already happened.

Approach #1 (recommended by Laurie Beth Jones, author of The Path):

It's the first week of ________ *(current month)*, **____ (+ 3 years from today)**...

____

____

____

____

____

____

____

____

____

____

Approach #2: Take each area of your life and write a detailed description of how that area will look at some point in the future - 2 years from now, 3 years from now or 5 years from now.

Career/business

Health/wellness

Finances

Spouse/significant other

Family & friends

Spiritual development

Professional development

Fun & recreation

Family & friends

Spiritual development

Professional development

Fun & recreation

Physical environment/home

Additional

GPS Tool For Tip #31: Skills Assessment Worksheet Taking Inventory Of Our Assets

How many years were you in the workforce?

____

What industry are your in? How many years were you in your industry?

____

What career level (individual contributor, supervisor, team leader, manager, director, VP, SVP, CEO) are you presently at?

____

How many years were you in your current position?

____

How much time has passed since your last promotion?

____

Is your resume up-to-date?

____

Do you possess sound interviewing skills?

____

Can you list out your key networking partnerships?

What degrees do you possess?

What degree coursework have you completed?

What certifications have you been awarded?

What professional development steps have you taken in the last five years?

____

____

____

____

____

____

Have you taken a Personality Assessment recently (Winslow, Myers Briggs, DiSC, Peoplemap, etc.)? If so, which one?

____

What is your Personality Type?

____

What are your Personality Strengths?

____

____

____

____

____

What are your Personality Weaknesses?

List your top 3 career values. Write a sentence or two about why this value is important to you.

Value #1:

Value #2:

Value #3:

Define your best "You" - complete the following sentence: When I'm running at peak performance…

What are your greatest lessons learned from your career?

Appendix 1: Recommended Reading

Visit www.TheGPSCoach.com and click on the Amazon icon for easy ordering.

The Path: Creating Your Mission Statement for Work and for Life by Laurie Beth Jones

Failing Forward by John C. Maxwell

Margin – Restoring Emotional, Physical, Financial and Time Reserves to Overloaded Lives by Richard A. Swenson, M.D.

Nice Girls Don't Get the Corner Office: 101 Unconscious Mistakes Women Make That Sabotage Their Careers by Lois P. Frankel, Ph.D

Change Your Questions, Change Your Life by Marliee G. Adams, Ph.D.

BRAG! The Art of Tooting Your Own Horn Without Blowing It by Peggy Klaus

Fierce Conversations – Achieving Success at Work & in Life, One Conversation at a Time by Susan Scott

30-Day Job Promotion – build a powerful promotion plan in a month by Susan Britton Whitcomb

The Christian's Career Journey – Finding the Job God Designed for You by Susan Britton Whitcomb

The Dream Giver by Bruce Wilkinson

Love it, Don't Leave it – 26 Ways to get what you want at Work by Beverly Kaye and Sharon Jordan-Evans

About The GPS Coaching Program

These are just some of the things people are saying about the GPS Coaching Program:

"Evelyn Kaufman is my life coach. Yeah, I know it sounds girly, but here is what she did. I had dreams and plans, but ***I was falling into the trap of "whatever makes a paycheck."*** *She helped me turn them into goals, and helped me* ***define and distill those goals.*** *By this, I mean I am no good with goals because they always end up being so far away. Well, she helped me take my long term goals, and create monthly, weekly, and even daily goals that all related to each other.* ***Every day I know what I have to do, and what it means for me to be successful today, this week, this month, and this year. It was the best investment in my business I ever made."*** — Harry, Software Developer & Business Owner- Kentucky

* * * * *

"I started working with Evelyn because I was unhappy in the career I'd chosen. ***Evelyn helped me identify career options that are in sync my core values, skills and natural talents.*** *I have a plan in place and am now in the process of pursuing my dream job!"* — Felecia, Personal Trainer – Kentucky

* * * * *

"I have come to realize as a result of your coaching that every problem DOES have a solution. We often feel "stuck" - that we can't move forward with our goals because of an obstacle that seems too big to overcome. *But if we have someone to help us deal with these obstacles one step at a time, then they don't seem so big after all!"* — Michele, Engineer – Colorado

* * * * *

"Evelyn provided me with the resources to set goals for my career and the confidence that I could achieve my dreams!" — Gina, Training Development Analyst – Kentucky

* * * * *

"Evelyn Kaufman is a Christ-centered, compassionate and gifted coach. With her warm and loving manner, she is able to guide and facilitate self discovery and clarify direction. I emerged from her program very clear on my mission and vision and with tremendous peace about my life. ***I recommend her program to anyone who has ever wanted more meaning and direction in their life." —*** Juliet, At Home Mom & Piano Teacher – Florida

* * * * *

Are You Ready To Get Started With GPS Coaching?

Visit our website at www.TheGPSCoach.com or email Evelyn@TheGPSCoach.com for a complimentary meeting to discuss your route and destination! While you are at my site, don't forget to sign up for your free gift (The GPS Career Assessment) and my no spam monthly newsletter.

Evelyn Kaufman

"My mission is to inspire, nurture, and encourage others toward greater insight."

In the area of teaching personal fulfillment and helping others to live a life they can be passionate about, Evelyn Kaufman is uniquely qualified. Evelyn is an energetic, yet thought provoking Coach having received training from the *Institute of Life Coach Training*, and the *Career Coach Academy*. She is a Certified Life Coach and Certified Career Management Coach. Evelyn over 20 years of progressive leadership in the corporate and business world and holds an MBA.

With a desire to help others be the best they can be, Evelyn created ***Journey to Fullness Inc.*** which provides career coaching to individuals in a variety of areas (i.e., career management, resume makeovers, job search strategy).

As a Workshop and Teleclass presenter she provides training on topics including *Effective Communication, Living Your Mission, Career Branding,* and *Avoiding Career Derailment.*

Her most recent development, the GPS Coaching Program, allows her to partner with professionals as they map out their ideal career plan.

Made in the USA
Monee, IL
04 November 2026

67378686R00059